*Too Licky* by Gigi Giles and Ryan Giles
Published by Too Licky LLC,
Jacksonville FL 32207
www.toolicky.com
www.facebook.com/toolickybook/
First Edition.

# FOREWORD

*Too Licky* is a perfect book to share the wonderful experience of rescuing a dog with your entire family. Socially conscious, adorable, and full of great imagery, *Too Licky* will make a great book to add to your classroom, shelter, and your personal collection. You have selected a book that not only shares the joy of rescuing a shelter dog, but this book also gives back to rescue and education-focused nonprofits in multiple communities. What more could you ask for?

Deirdre 'Little Darling' Franklin
President/CEO of Pinups for Pitbulls, Inc.
and author of *Little Darling's Pinups for Pitbulls: A Celebration of America's Most Lovable Dogs and The Pit Bull Life: A Dog Lover's Companion*

# FOREWORD

This book promises to be a little gem, a beautiful, simple, touching reminder that shelters have a perfect dog for everyone.

## By Sophie Gamand

Sophie Gamand is a French award-winning photographer and animal advocate. Sophie travels around the U.S. photographing shelter dogs for free, to help bring awareness to their fate, and help them get adopted. Her most known series are *Wet Dog* and *Flower Power, Pit Bulls of the Revolution.*

She has won several prestigious photography awards for her work (including a Sony World Photography Award in 2014), as well as advocacy awards for her dedication to animal rescue and adoption.

# FOREWORD

Monroe was the first dog I adopted 21 years ago. He was a mischievous Basenji mix that changed my life all for the better, and was my first insight into the millions of homeless dogs who need forever homes.

Dogs are with us for such a brief time, but during that time, they live and love large with unrivaled loyalty. Maybe that's why it hurts so much when they part from this earth. Each of my dogs has inspired me in one way or another to save, foster or adopt another dog. It kills me when I hear people say, "I just can't have another dog. It hurts too much." There are SO many amazing, homeless dogs that deserve love. In return, your heart will heal and grow larger.

Welcoming a dog into your family is a forever commitment that you will never regret. Long after they are gone from this earth, they remain part of us, and continue to bring out the good and compassion in us.

## By Tes M. Kurtz

Tes M. Kurtz is an award-nominated marketing content writer. She also wrote *Anything Is PAWSible—Impossible Dog Dreams Come True.* You can follow Tes and her dog adventures on Instagram: rescuedogwriter.

# ILLUSTRATOR PREFACE

My daughter, Jillienne, and I are avid rescue advocates who have a passion for fostering shelter dogs and finding them loving, forever homes. From a very young age, Jillienne loved bully breeds and always wanted to be an 'end of life' foster for a dog with terminal illness. On November 16, 2015, both of her wishes came true when we became foster parents for Trucker, a six-year-old Pitbull mix who was brought into Clay County Animal Care and Control as a stray. Thanks to the shelter's compassionate vet, Dr. Jennifer Broadhurst and FOCCA, a volunteer organization that pays for the medical treatment of the shelter animals, Trucker was not euthanized and was given a second chance. This sweet little lowrider was diagnosed with Mast Cell Cancer and Advanced Heartworm Disease and simply needed a loving home to live out the remainder of his days.

We fell in love immediately with Trucker's gentle demeanor, adorable grunts and grin that made everyone smile. We created a Facebook page for him appropriately named "Trucker's Bucket List" and began our journey of giving Trucker the life he deserved. From beach visits to special treats, we wanted to make his remaining time with us as special as possible. But Trucker had a different plan and decided that he wasn't ready to leave us any time soon. In March of 2016, his vet told us that he was doing so well on his medication that he could possibly live another two to three years! As much as we loved him, we knew that this boy deserved a forever family of his own. So, we began our journey to find a home for a six-year-old Pitbull who had heartworm disease and cancer.

We were not entirely optimistic that we would find someone who would be willing to adopt a dog that may or may not be a part of their lives for very long, but once again, Trucker proved us wrong. Everyone who met Trucker fell in love with him. He had such a special way of drawing people to him. Three different families wanted to adopt him, but each one fell through. We were becoming discouraged, but on May 21st, Jillienne decided to take him to an adoption event. It was there that he met an incredible family who fell for him instantly. He did a sleepover at their home that evening and found

his forever home! He spent his days basking in the sun, sniffing the warm breeze off the lake and spent his nights snuggled in his human sister's bed. His family adored him and continued to share his journey via his Facebook page.

Sadly, just six months later, on Thanksgiving weekend, Trucker unexpectedly became very ill and the Morales family helped him cross the Rainbow Bridge. For just a little over one year, Trucker touched so many lives, made so many people smile and was an incredible ambassador for his breed. Trucker was the sweetest, most loving dog we have ever fostered, despite the mistreatment he experienced at the hands of his former owners. The illustration of him sticking his tongue out while Jillienne kissed his head was based on a photo taken at the dog park, and it was also the inspiration for the name of this book, "Too Licky".

As I painted the illustrations for this book and read each dog's story, my mind kept wandering back to Trucker. A dog that most people would overlook provided so much joy and love to so many people. I encourage you to visit your local shelter and adopt a dog rather than purchasing one. Shelter and rescue dogs seem to have an innate sense that they have been saved and have a special way of changing your life. I also encourage you to get involved with your local shelter or rescue organization.

As the illustrator of Too Licky, I hope to honor Trucker's memory, and dedicate this book to all of the shelter dogs who are still waiting for their forever homes.

Cynthia Inks

# AUTHOR PREFACE

We love dogs!

Big ones, small ones, fluffy ones and even ones that are too licky!

When our family was ready to get a dog, we knew we'd adopt one from a shelter.

Adopting a dog from a shelter can be overwhelming.

We were lucky to have the help of a local rescue dog advocate, Cynthia. Cynthia not only helped us find the 'perfect' rescue dog, Sugar, she also taught us a lot.

That's why we wanted to include TIPS for adopting the 'just right' rescue to help other families adopt dogs that need rescuing.

During our search for the 'perfect' rescue dog, we learned a lot about the organizations who help shelter dogs. Like, *Friends of Clay County Animals, Inc.* (FOCCA) who pays for the medical bills for dogs at the shelter where we adopted Sugar, and Pit Sisters that has this cool program called *TAILS* (Teaching Animals & Inmates Life Skills) where they bring together hard-to-adopt shelter dogs with inmates—transforming their lives.

We also learned about the discrimination some breeds face and the organizations that help these dogs. Like, *Pinups for Pitbulls, Inc.* that educates the public about pitbull-type dogs and raises awareness to fight against laws that discriminate against them.

With this book, we will support organizations that help care for dogs in shelters as well as those that advocate for bully breeds.

We are grateful and proud to feature 21 dogs from the rescue dog community as the illustrations for our book. We're also grateful to their furever families for sharing their rescue stories with us to include in our book. We hope their stories will inspire others to adopt a rescue dog.

We believe every dog deserves love and a loving home.

Gigi Giles & Ryan Giles
(Edited by our mom, Jody Giles)

This book is dedicated to all the dogs sleeping in a shelter tonight.

May they find their furever home.

Gigi and Ryan lived in California.

One day their mom and dad said, "Guess what? We are moving to Florida AND we are getting a dog!"

Of course, Gigi and Ryan only heard "we are getting a dog!"

After Gigi and Ryan had settled into their new home, the search for the perfect dog began...

Gigi said, this dog is...
TOO BIG

Ryan said, this dog is...
Too small

Gigi said, this dog is...
Too fast

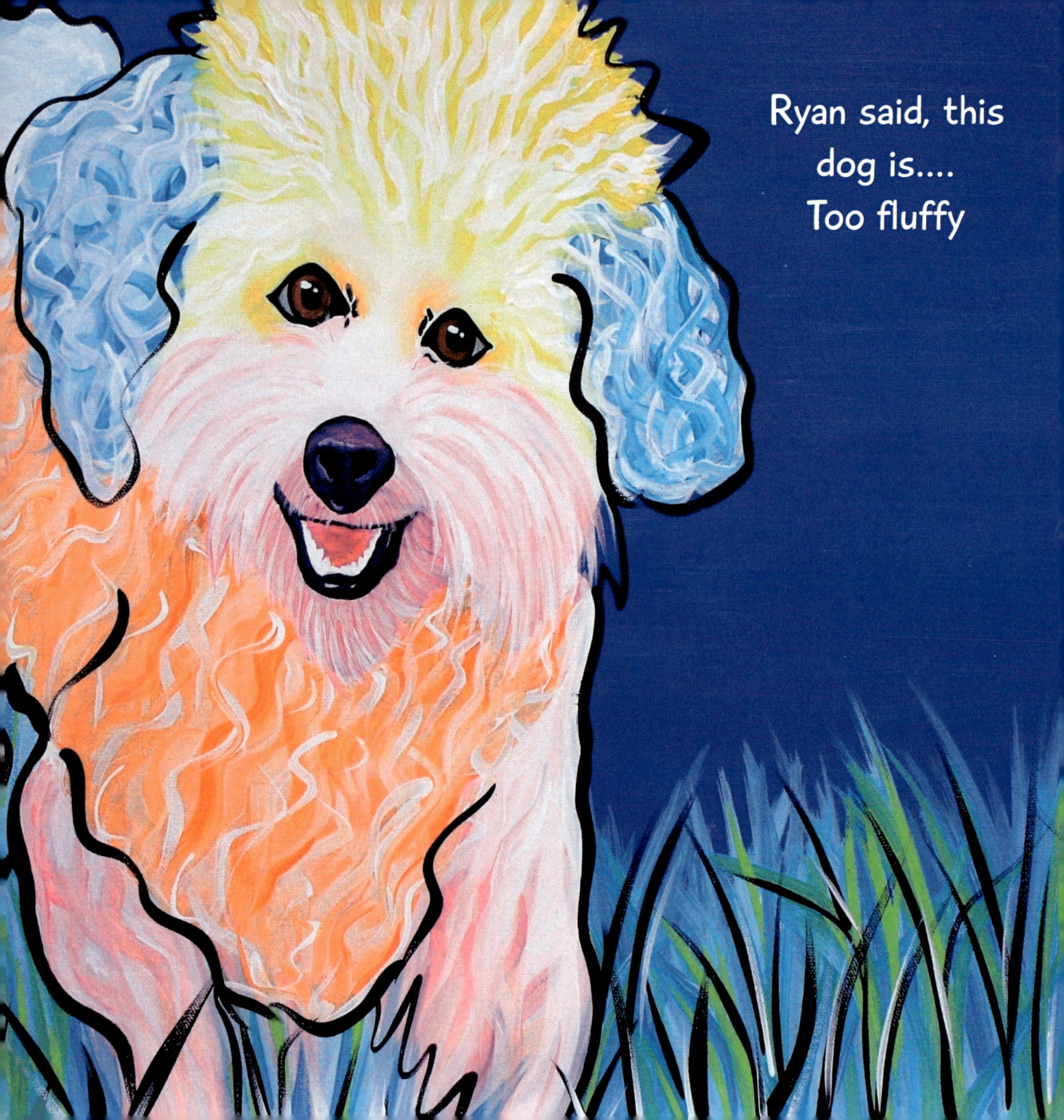

Ryan said, this dog is....
Too fluffy

Gigi said, this
dog is...
Too puppy

Gigi said, this dog is...
Too wolfy

Ryan said, this dog is...
Too spotty

Gigi said, this dog is...
Too serious

Ryan said, this dog is...
Too weinery

Gigi said, this dog is...
Too LICKY

Ryan said, this dog is...
Too foxy

Gigi said, this dog is...
Too wrinkly

Ryan said,
this dog is...
Too scruffy

Gigi said, this dog
is...
Too drooly

Ryan said, this dog is...
Too toothy

Gigi said, this dog is...
Too distracted

Ryan said, this dog is...
Too tiger-y

Gigi said, these dogs are...
Too silly

Ryan said, this dog is...
Too tongue-y

Gigi said, this dog
is...
Too goofy

Ryan said, this dog is...
Too squishy

Then a friend
suggested they go
to the shelter.

And they met Sugar.
Sugar was perfect.

Alexis Kyle Suttles
Allison Cohen
Amelia Bond
Animal Lover in Cleveland
Anne Bosse
Audrey and Kate Brice
B Torkko
Barbara N. Clarke
Byrdie, Woodson and Lane Bailey
Carol Cotterly for Spencer, Conway & Hank
Carolyn Cantrell Snowden, Jacksonville Dog Café
Carrie Denny
Christine, Colette and Dodger
Cindy Frick
Cindy H Chism
Connie Cannaday, The London Sanctuary
Constance Mullins
Cynthia Haberman
Dale Mocalkins
Dan, Kathy, Jaren, & Michele Sykora
Darcy, Fred, Sophie Anne and Jellybean
Debbie Giles Spies
Diana & Giovanni Manzano in honor of Skippy The Tripawd
Diana Feyes
Don M
Double Doggie
Eileen Kennedy
Elizabeth Stepanek in honor of sweet Nova
Eva and Perry Rogers
Fran Hutchins
Gabriel R.
GommyOnyx
Heather Henderson
Helen Michelle Dobson
Holdorff family

Jack & Chloe Bartley
Jaime Kelsey
Jamye, Sean and George Phillips
Jeannie Weenie
Jeff Bryan
Jeff Suttles
Jenni Beck
Jennifer Korber and James Korber
Jessica Dalton
Julie, Daizey & Donavon Beatty
Kaitlyn Easterling
Kate, Lawrence, and Sonny Cevallos
Kelly Watson
Kevin Abbott
Kim Pinkham
Kizzie, Koko, Kia and Kazz's Mom, Cindi Miller Herleman

# KICKSTARTER PAWRAISERS

Laura Turner
Lauren Greenwade
Lauren O'Connell
Laurie Deemer
Lema & Willa Smith
Lisa Blount
Lisa Klink
Liv and Elin Broner
Liz Behnisch
Lori Beck
Lynn Baird
Maggi Suttles
Mallory Bennin and Blanco
Margaret T. Eighan
Megan M Miller
Michael Deegan
Mike Santos

Mineca Riggs
Morgan Elliott
Nancy Lynn Horton
Nibs, Leeloo and Charlotte Rasmussen
Nicholas Savaiano
Nikki and Bobbi
Peggy Blackwelder
Pup Package
Reid family
Rescue Me Pet Clothing
Rob Giles family
Rufus' mom
Ryleigh Harris
Sarah and Jonathan Helms
Savy Leiser
Scooter Perlstein and Family
Shannon Hainline
Shelly Thorburn
Sheri Inks
Stella L. Kerch
Stephanie, Wilbur & Emma Tufts
Story, Max, Howie, and Betsy
Sue Haslam
Summer May McCudden
Tes M. Kurtz
The Calvino family
The Camerlengo Family
The Cooks kids: Kessandra, Cheyenne, Michael & Cameron
The Sweet Family
The Sasser Family
Theresa Amy
Tracy Pellicer - Furrie Fotographie

# Stories of Featured Rescue Dogs

### TOO BIG, BIG BEN

Ben was our first rescue dog. He had been dropped off at the Humane Society and clearly showed signs of neglect. Thankfully, the Saint Bernard Rescue picked him up right away.

We had lost our first dog and were so incredibly heartbroken as our dog was very young and it was not expected. The woman who runs the Saint Bernard Rescue was a friend and she said she had the perfect dog for us. His name was Ben. Ben is so full of love and is excellent with kids. And, kids sure do love him! He is 180 pounds of pure love.

### TOO SMALL, SKIPPY

Skippy is a special, special-needs dog. He's a 2 1/2-pound Chihuahua with barely any hair and three legs. He was born with a birth deformity yet, he still can do almost everything other dogs can do. He has his own little ways of communicating what he wants, when he wants it.

Skippy was rescued from a backyard breeder's home, and now fills our home with pure love.

### TOO FAST, BELLA

In October 2012, I came across a post on Facebook that said our local city shelter was packed to the gills and needed fosters. I looked through the album of dogs in need of fostering and saw this cute four-month-old puppy. She had an upper respiratory infection and needed to get out of the shelter to heal. I wondered how she got there all alone and what she had been through in her short life of only four months.

When I first laid eyes on her I knew, I was in trouble. She was adorable!

But, I already had three dogs. This one, whom we named Bella, we were intending to just foster…to save a life.

We made an adoption flyer and took Bella on several outings. As time passed, we knew we couldn't let her go. We knew she was a part of our family so we decided to adopt her. Since, Bella has been an ambassador for her breed. She has her Canine Good Citizen® training. When Bella and I were turned away from a local event because of her breed, we stood up to the Jacksonville Beach city officials with the help of Pit Sisters. Now, you cannot have an event in Jacksonville beach that excludes any breed of dogs. Bella wants to end BSL! Every dog deserves love. Regardless of breed.

### TOO SPOTTY, BARKLEY

Barkley was rescued after following children to a school bus. Rescue Adoptions found him and I adopted him in October 2016, the weekend after Hurricane Matthew hit. We realize he could have been stuck out in the storm, but thankfully he was found just in time!

Although we got Barkley for our daughter who is on the Autism spectrum, he has stolen all of our hearts. Barkley really is her best friend. He instantly knew she was unique and loves her dearly.

We are dumbfounded as to why anyone would've given up this little guy. When we got Barkley, he was skittish and had numerous scars (presumably from abuse). The most amazing thing is how quickly and easily he released his past and was able to open up to our daughter. It really is an amazing bond.

### TOO FANCY, MADDOX

Maddox is our rescue dog from Puerto Rico. My husband was working in the rainforest when this little puppy found him. One phone call and I was smitten! Then, $100 and three days later this little Sato was flown to Tennessee. We had to work through a lot of issues when he first came to our home, but within the year we welcomed our first daughter and his demeanor completely changed.

Everyone says this, but he truly is the BEST dog there ever was. Calm, patient and loving. Clearly, he is easy going as he's pictured wearing a princess dress for a tea party!

### TOO FLUFFY, PROFESSOR

In 2007, I received an email forwarded to me from a friend who was highly involved in the local shelter and rescue. It showed photos of a very depressed "Poodle," who wasn't handling shelter life very well and needed a home as the end of his time was near. He had been found wandering in a field so matted and dirty that he had to be shaved. He looked sad and naked! I sent my now husband to the shelter because I was sure I'd have to take every animal home if I went. He described walking past all the happy bouncing balls of fur to the last cage, where he found a dog that looked sick. Professor wouldn't look at him. My husband came home to get me and our other dog so we could see how they would do together.

As soon as Professor was brought out of his cage into the meet-and-greet area he was like a new dog! Smiling and sitting up! Excited as he could be to meet us and our other dog! So, guess who came home with us that day? Over time his very fluffy fur grew back in and we discovered he is really a Bichon. We tend to keep his fur short, but he's quite fluffy if we let it grow. Professor's now a sweet old man at 17 years old. He's been an amazing doggy over the years!

### TOO PUPPY, JELLY BEAN

Jelly Bean's momma was hours away from being euthanized while VERY pregnant. She was rescued at the last possible moment, and three days later had nine pups! We are so fortunate to have one of those perfect little pups. Jelly Bean was one pound when she became a part of our family.

We may have rescued her at the start, but she has rescued us many times over. We are truly blessed to have her in our family and she is our daughter's best friend.

### TOO WOLFY, QUEZY

In May 1999, I went to our local shelter to find a friend for our dog, Max, who was adopted from the same shelter three months prior. As I scanned row after row of dogs, one little six-month-old stray caught my eye. We went in to the meet-and-greet area, and she jumped on the table and peed on my purse. I was hooked. She had green stuff coming out of her nose, which the staff worker told me meant she'd have to be put in isolation. Isolation dogs rarely made it out at that time. I scrambled and received permission to take her to my vet. We went home, crossed our fingers and began our story.

We named her after Jacquez Green—the football player who could run like no other. Quezy was a force to be reckoned with. Wild, untamed and full of fire. She would catch birds midair, take squirrels off fences and dig out of holes made for mice. She took every opportunity to escape and would always be found running covered in mud and smiling ear to ear. She could run so far and jump so high that I truly think sometimes she caught flight. She gave me gray hair and wrinkles, and more joy and love than anyone could imagine. She moved with me countless times, and welcomed every new foster and permanent addition not with happiness, but with acceptance and peace. She rolled with the changes life brought us. When human children came into the picture, a kinder, softer side of Quezy emerged. She would lick their tiny feet and stare at them in wonder. That was when she fell in love.

We celebrated her 17th adoption anniversary in May 2016. We had to hold her to help her walk and we sat with her in the shade as she laid down eating her cake. Her body may have finally failed her, but the glimmer in her eyes never left. She was an old lady who sat looking at each of us with a smile that said more than words ever could. We knew that we had made her as happy as she had made us. A couple of weeks later life became too hard and with our help, The Wild Child, our restless wanderer, slept at last.

## TOO SERIOUS, ABBY

In February 2017, on one of the coldest days of the year, my daughter, Jillienne, called me while she was volunteering at the shelter. She was concerned about a senior dog named Abby, who was heartworm positive, had developed a respiratory infection and was not doing well. The volunteers were concerned about her handling the freezing temperatures. Jillienne asked if I could help find someone to foster her.

I immediately thought of my neighbor Julie, who mentioned that she would like to try fostering. As I told her about Abby, she didn't hesitate to say that she would take her in. Just a few hours later, Abby was transported to Julie's house. Julie and her children fell in love with Abby and their dog, George, welcomed her into their home. Abby quickly became accustomed to spending her days sunbathing or curled up in Julie's home office. She was a trooper as she went through her heartworm treatment and enjoyed daily walks with her foster brother. After falling in love, Julie and her family adopted Abby. She fit perfectly into their family.

Abby finally learned what it was like to feel the love and kindness she deserved. As Abby's health began to deteriorate, Julie and her family helped Abby make her way to the Rainbow Bridge where they are certain she is restored to her youth.

I'm grateful to Julie that Abby lived her final days in a warm, loving home.

## TOO WEINERY / DAX

Dax was found wandering around west of Jacksonville. His rescuers put out signs for a few weeks, but no one responded. They needed to find someone to re-home him because they already had several dogs of their own.

A friend, who knows I'm a dachshund lover, forwarded Dax's information to me and I fell for him instantly! Through the help of friends and rescue advocates, Dax made the journey to Key West and he's been here ever since!

Dax spends most days on our boat or in the water. As his illustration suggests, he's loves life in the Keys!

## TOO WRINKLY, BLONDIE

Blondie was rescued as a very young pup. Her eyes weren't even open. She was surrendered to the Humane Society with her siblings and they needed a foster to bottle feed them. After raising Blondie and two of her other siblings until they were old enough to be adopted, I could not part with this little girl and we adopted her. Blondie is "Too Wrinkly" because she's part Lab and Shar Pei, and as a puppy she was totally covered in adorable wrinkles!

Blondie has been my constant, loyal and loving companion for the past seven years. She inspired me to continue to foster and I have had over 100 animals in my home over the years, until they were adopted into loving families. Blondie even inspired me to start my own nonprofit rescue organization called Rescue Junkie. Since we started in 2014, we have seen nearly 500 animals adopted through our rescue.

## TOO FOXY, GRACIE

My neighbors found a lost dog and did not realize she was pregnant. Gracie was number seven of her litter. Her mom did not have a tit for her, so my neighbor's husband hand fed her. That's why she loves people so much! When I came to visit the pups, Gracie walked into my palm—and my heart—forever. She rescued me!

## TOO SCRUFFY, SCOOTER

We rescued Scooter when he was shoved through the gate and into the fenced yard of some elderly neighbors. Thankfully the neighbor called us to come get him from her yard. Scooter was very scared, but we were able to coax him with bits of chicken and bring him home. He is still afraid of everything. But, he is ours and he is loved.

## TOO DROOLY, FIONA

Fiona was a stray in Miami-Dade county. She was brought in by Animal Care and Control with a fresh litter of pups. The puppies adopted out fast, and Fiona even found a home, too. Because she had just had puppies, her new parents were to bring her back to be spayed after she recovered. Well, they brought her in, but never came back to pick her up. Once again, she was up for adoption. This time she found a loving home, but her anxiety was

# Stories of Featured Rescue Dogs

full blown. She kept running away. Again, she was returned to Miami-Dade pound. When I went to pick her up, she had days left before she would be euthanized.

When she came to my home she was very lethargic and moppy. She would rearrange my house if I left her home alone. So, I brought her with me everywhere until she livened up a bit. Then, I introduced her to a crate, which she loves. I call it her room. It gave her a safe space while I was away at work. Other than work, she came with me and was my shotgun rider in the truck.

Now, six years later she has two human sisters and is living the life! We have our ups and downs, but she was and will always be my first baby. I couldn't ask for a better dog!

## TOO TOOTHY, ROCKY

We moved our family from Connecticut to south Florida and told our kids, Jaren and Michele, that once we bought our new house we would get a dog. We found Pet Haven Rescue from an internet search and a couple of pictures caught our eye. Rocky had been born at the rescue facility and was a true mutt: Shih Tzu, Pug and Poodle mix. He was the only one in his litter that ended up looking like he did. All his siblings looked more like mama Poodle. We loved his funny teeth and he was a very calm dog. He had already been adopted and was returned a month after his adoption because the man, a church pastor, was having problems with his knees and was afraid he wouldn't be able to take Rocky on walks. He prayed that a nice family with a large yard and fence would end up adopting the dog. We happen to have a very large yard and a fence for Rocky! The funny thing is that Rocky goes and hides whenever anyone mentions the "walk" word. He is a homebody. And, the best dog we've ever had!

## TOO DISTRACTED, TRAVIS

In December, my daughter was working on a 20-hour project called "Paw Presents". She set up collection boxes at a local pet store to collect old, gently-used items to bring to the Humane Society. One Saturday, a rescue group was there with dogs needing homes. They set up right next to my daughter's collection box. Travis was one of the dogs there that day.

Before Travis and his brother, Jake, were saved by Rescue Adoption they were living outside crammed in a dog pen with A LOT of other dogs, and not much human contact. Certainly, not any loving human contact. Travis was beat down, extremely submissive and would cower at every person.

A man and woman whose dog recently passed were loving on Travis looking for a dog to save as their house was now empty. My daughter and I couldn't help but encourage this couple to adopt Travis. You could just tell that Travis was a wonderful dog and he deserved a loving home, and these people were the real deal. They filled out adoption papers and I was so thrilled that Travis was going home. My daughter put Travis on her lap while the couple roamed around the store looking for some items to get him for his new home. A bit later, the man tapped me on the shoulder to tell me that his wife left the store in tears. She just wasn't ready for another dog. His wife told him

to go back inside and tell me that unfortunately, they were not going to adopt Travis. But, if we wanted him, we should take him home. The man said his wife saw how much my daughter and I cared for Travis. And because they weren't ready, they wanted him to go home with us.

Travis is the perfect little companion dog and always a show stopper!

## TOO TIGER-Y, JAGGER

Jagger is a Pitbull mix that had been living on a chain and without food before I adopted him. Although he was only eight months old, my veterinarian thought he was a senior. He was covered in fleas and emaciated. He was unable to walk on his hind legs due to malnutrition. He started gaining weight as soon as I started feeding him. Once he was fed a proper diet, he could walk on his hind legs.

I fostered Jagger until he was adopted.

Jagger was adopted out twice. The first family kept him until the husband had to move out of town for work and the wife did not want the responsibility of caring for Jagger. The second family, well, let's just say that Jagger ended up at our local shelter twice. They did not want to claim him after he got out of their fence the second time.

This sweet boy was adopted a third time by Emma Watson. For Jagger, Emma is an angel from Heaven. From the first time she met him, she knew they had a special connection. Emma adopted Jagger and the two became inseparable. Due to Emma putting a lot of time into his obedience training, Jagger is now a well-rounded dog. I am so thankful for Emma for adopting Jagger and giving him a loving forever home.

To this day, I receive photo and video updates of Jagger. He also gets to share his life with several dogs and a cat.

## TOO SILLY, CHANCE & PARKER

Chance and I fell in love at first sight. An Australian Kelpie mix, I adopted him Oct 8, 2004 from Noah's Bark Rescue in Manhattan Beach, CA. He was just under two years old and quick to adore my seven-pound Papillon, Filbert. Chance weighed 42 pounds, but was convinced he was as petite as his brother. Despite being oblivious to his size, Chance was an extremely bright, highly energetic love, who was too silly for his own good. He would run full speed across a room and crash into the wall as he turned to race up the stairs. When I was away, he entertained himself by ripping up my carpet. On a walk, he attempted to herd my neighborhood priest and nipped him in the ankle. I almost sent Chance back, but decided this working dog needed to work. We went to training classes together, and he developed hobbies to release that smart, silly energy every day. He was my running partner, herded other dogs at the dog park or beach, and played Frisbee and fetch.

On Sep 21, 2008, my family was playing ball at a neighborhood park. A stray dog came out of nowhere and immediately attached to Chance. The Corgi-Chihuahua mix wouldn't let a human come within three feet of him, but he ran around the park with Chance for two hours and followed us home. Sometimes you pick your dog. Sometimes your dog picks you. Other times,

# Stories of Featured Rescue Dogs

your dog picks your other dog. Parker picked Chance.

Filbert passed away one month later. Chance was devastated and found comfort with Parker, whose personality blossomed into a clown dog. They became inseparable, bonded boys. It takes silly to know silly, and this silly duo made me laugh every single day!

Parker and I lost Chance on Jan 3, 2016, leaving us heartbroken. To alleviate Parker's loneliness, I adopted laid-back Hazel from A Purposeful Rescue in Los Angeles on May 15, 2016. Parker's carrying on the legacy and teaching her all kinds of silly.

### TOO TONGUE-Y, ELSIE

Elsie was on the kill list at a shelter in Alabama. She was pregnant at the time, and rescued by Big Dog Ranch just in time to save her life and the lives of her babies. My son, Ethan, was looking for a puppy and fell in love when he saw Elsie, who was two at the time. She scaled half a tree chasing a lizard, and he was sold! I was unsure at the time, but I'm so thankful, now. She is the sweetest, most amazingly loving dog. She's been such a blessing in our lives! And... she just happened to have my great grandmother's name!

### TOO GOOFY, CHARLIE

We adopted Charlie from a coworker when he was just under one-year old. He had apparently been nothing but trouble for the family. They showed me photos of their bedroom door torn to shreds, toilet paper all over the house, and even shared numerous stories of his destruction. She mentioned that they were getting rid of him and were looking for a family. My family had 100% agreed to not allow any more animals into the house. But, my father surprised us and took me to formally meet Charlie. We met at a park and I asked why we were meeting him. I was told, "He's ours." We've had Charlie for seven years now and have had zero issues with him—other than the occasional trash can digging. He is my best friend and the sweetest goof I've ever known. Adopting him was the best decision this family made!

### TOO SQUISHY, SNOW

I was a new volunteer at Clay County Animal Care and Control. Snow came in as an approximately six-year-old stray with two puppies. The shelter was packed and I only volunteered a couple times a week, so the next time I saw her, she was coming out of surgery. It was the end of the day and she didn't look like she was feeling well. Her puppies had been adopted, so she would have been alone for the weekend at a county shelter. The other volunteer, Cynthia, and I instantly fell in love with her. She was so sweet, adorable and quite pitiful coming out of anesthesia. Cynthia had a foster at the time, but said she could foster Snow—and was even interested in adopting her—once she placed the other foster. I had never fostered before, but knowing I had a backup foster, decided to take her home.

We didn't know it, but Snow had acquired an URI and was SO sick for a couple of weeks. We nursed her back to health. A few weeks later, Cynthia messaged me on Facebook because she had placed her foster and was ready for Snow to go live with her. I suddenly became very emotional and

couldn't even pick up the phone to call her. I was on the computer and Snow was sitting up on the edge of the couch staring at me. The thought of making her feel any sense of abandonment once again just overwhelmed me.

Being the professional foster that she is, Cynthia realized that I was upset and told me if I wanted to adopt her, I should. It took me three seconds to decide that Snow needed to stay. I loved her so much and couldn't imagine losing her and making her lose us, even though I knew she would have an AMAZING home with Cynthia. So, I became a proud foster failure!

Sadly, about a year after having her, Snow was diagnosed with Stage 4 lymphoma. She was given 4 weeks to live without chemo, so we went the chemo route. After more than two rounds of chemo and 14 months later, we lost her. I was holding her and telling her how much I loved her when she left this earth. She passed on her own, two hours before Laps of Love arrived. I only had the pleasure of loving her for two and half years, but the love I have for her is as strong as the love I have for dogs that were with me for 17 years. We bonded fast and deeply through her sickness. I mourn her every day and am so grateful for the opportunity I had to love her. She was an amazing dog and friend!

I recently fostered and failed, again. I knew going into it that I would most likely fail, so I was prepared. Some people can foster and some just can't. There is no other love that can compare to the unconditional love you get from a dog....and it seems magnified when it's a true rescue. They just seem to know you changed their life forever and are eternally grateful.

# TIPS FOR FINDING THE "JUST RIGHT" RESCUE

## Tip 1 Before you begin your search, what kind of dog are you looking for?

Having an idea of the type of dog you are looking for is tremendously helpful before you begin your search. When we started our search, an adoption expert asked us some wonderful probing questions that helped us gain a better idea of the type of dog we wanted. All that said, it's important to note that no matter how much you've narrowed down your "type," it's likely to change after your journey begins.

Here are 7 great questions to consider:

1. **What is the 'right' size?** This one is fairly straightforward, but having a size in mind is really helpful. Do you want a smaller lap dog, a mid-size (20-40 pounds) dog or a large dog (over 40 pounds)?

2. **What is the 'right' fur type?** For our family, fur type was part of our search criteria as my husband and daughter have allergies. However, we did learn from dog experts that after 2-3 weeks of the dog in your home, most human's allergies acclimate. The other consideration regarding fur type is home maintenance. Most dogs shed. Is there one type of fur over another you'd prefer cleaning up?

3. **What is the 'right' activity level (for you and your new best friend)?** How much exercise do you currently get? How much exercise do you plan on allowing your dog to get? Some dogs require more exercise than other. It's good to consider how much time you have in your day to walk and play with your furry friend.

4. **What is the 'right' age?** Puppy, young adult, middle-aged, senior. It is easy to get sucked into the puppy craze, however dog experts and shelter volunteers like to remind adopters of the very short window a puppy is a puppy. Not to mention, a puppy takes extra commitment. On the other side of the coin, older dogs are generally well housebroken, tend to be more settled and calm, and are usually easy to take for walks.

5. **How much time to do you want to devote to training?** Most training time is required on the front end if your new pup needs some training with walking on leash, sitting, recall (coming when called) or house-training. Being consistent with training and devoting the time to it is important. Having an idea of how much training you're willing to take on will guide you in asking the probing questions to the shelter staff about how much training may be required with a certain candidate.

6. **What is the 'right' breed?** There are generally two types; purebred and mixed breed. Most shelters have plenty of both.

Purebred rescue: With a purebred, you can research to learn about their temperament and disposition. You're also likely to have a good idea of their full-grown size. If you are unable to find the breed you're looking for at a shelter, type the breed name and the word "rescue" into your Internet search engine. You'll find a number of rescue groups around the country. (lab rescue, pug rescue, shaggy dog rescue, etc.)

Mixed breed: With a mixed bred, you'll have your own unique bred. And, you can still research the combination of the different identified breeds. Many believe that mixed bred dogs make the best pets because they are a combination of great traits from the breeds in their make-up. It is also believed that mixed breeds are likely to be healthier as they are free of genetic defects common to certain purebred dogs because of overbreeding.

## Tip 2 Keep an open mind regarding breeds – even Pit bulls, yes Pit bulls!

Pit bulls occupy almost 90 percent of the animal shelters across the country. William Berloni, director of dog training at The Humane Society of New York says, "The No. 1 trait in Pit bulls is loyalty to their guardians" and "these great dogs deserve to have devoted, caring owners who are worthy of that intense loyalty." Berloni says, "Pit bulls get a bad rap because of irresponsible owners."

If you are open to adopting a Pit bull, find out as much as you can from the shelter volunteers about the dog's history and what they know about his or her temperament.

## Tip 3 How to have a successful shelter search

### Spend time with dog

Remember, dogs are typically stressed out in a shelter setting and are not able to exhibit their true colors. The stress can manifest in fear, hyperactive or aggressive behavior. Ask the shelter staff if there's a space away from the noise where you can spend some time together. Also ask if you can take her for a walk. Cesar Milan says, "you can learn a great deal about a dog's energy and personality during a 10-minute walk."

### Ask the experts!

Ask the shelter volunteers for information on dogs. They work and play with the dogs on a daily basis and get to know the dog's personalities and tendencies. We were able to learn from shelter volunteers which dogs did well with children, other dogs, as well as the ones that walked well on a leash. They can usually also provide a good idea regarding the dog's activity level – from super active to the more mellow dogs.

### Take a trainer with you, if possible

If you have the luxury, take a dog trainer with you to help access the dogs. They are trained to evaluate behavior including a dog's body language, how he responds to being touched, how excitable he is, how quickly he calms down, how rough or gently he is in play, his reactions to other dogs, how he reacts if approached when he is eating or chewing on a toy, and how he responds to being startled. (Note, these are also the things you can ask the shelter volunteers.)

**Bring the whole family & any family dogs**

It is important that everyone in the home is on board with the idea of getting a new dog. Take the family when you go to the shelter including your current dog. Most shelters are familiar with handling these introductions.

**Ask the shelter staff if any rescues are currently in foster homes**

This is a great way to learn a lot about a rescue, as they've likely been in a home setting for days, if not, weeks. The foster parent should be able to tell you about the dog's temperament, how he reacts to other dogs, if he's been around children, and whether he's house trained.

**An insider tip from Cesar Milan about visiting hours at animal shelters**

Cesar recommends avoiding rush hour at the shelter, which tend to be weekends and afternoons. You may find a dog is more agitated than he would be when the shelter isn't so crowded with visitors. Cesar suggests going in the middle of the week. It's often slower and you'll be able to spend as much time as you need to make sure the dog you're considering is a good fit.

**LASTLY, use your instincts**

Listen to your instincts. It's likely you'll know when you see the dog that's meant for you.